SCHIRMER'S LIBRARY
OF MUSICAL CLASSICS

J. J. F. DOTZAUER

Exercises for Violoncello

Progressively arranged,
edited and fingered by

J. KLINGENBERG

➤ Book I: Nos. 1-34 — Library Vol. 1273

Book II: Nos. 35-62 — Library Vol. 1274

ISBN 978-0-7935-9148-0

G. SCHIRMER, *Inc.*

DISTRIBUTED BY

HAL•LEONARD®
CORPORATION

7777 W. BLUEMOUND RD. P.O. BOX 13819 MILWAUKEE, WI 53213

PREFACE

Since their appearance, the Violoncello Études by Dotzauer—who was born June 26, 1783, and died March 6, 1860—have ranked high among works of their class and, by reason of their intrinsic practical utility, have successfully maintained their position. It therefore seems entirely justifiable to bring out a new edition in line with modern requirements.

Dotzauer's numerous études are an outgrowth of mature experience in teaching, and display such a full and comprehensive understanding of the peculiarities of the instrument, that their well-earned place in the literature of violoncello-instruction would seem to be assured for the future also.

After careful consideration I reached the conclusion that a satisfactory new edition would be something different, in many respects, from a mere reprint of the original editions. I felt that the usefulness of these Études under present conditions would be greatly enhanced by a judicious selection from and rearrangement of the great mass of material; numerous mistakes had to be corrected, numbers of comparatively small value and utility had to be eliminated, and those of real importance and usefulness arranged in progressive order and clear classification, so that the present edition might be used as a supplement to any and every Method for Violoncello. My aim being not merely to promote technical efficiency, but to refine the taste and increase the capacity for shading and diversifying the tone, I have added—besides the needful fingerings, directions for the portions of the bow to be employed, and the establishment of the correct notation—marks of interpretation (expression and tempo) throughout; these latter, in earlier editions, were almost entirely wanting.

I hope that these admirable Études may now go forth in this more attractive garb, to promote and facilitate the difficult study of the Violoncello. JOHANNES KLINGENBERG.

Contents

Book 1 (Nos. 1-34)

Signs and Abbreviations

⊓   Down - Bow

V   Up - Bow

WB   Whole Bow

UH   Upper Half of Bow

LH   Lower Half of Bow

N   At the Nut

M   Middle of Bow

Pt.   At the Point

⌐‾‾‾   **Keep the finger on the note indicated until the line ends**

113 Études for Violoncello

Friedrich Dotzauer. Book I, Nos. 1-34

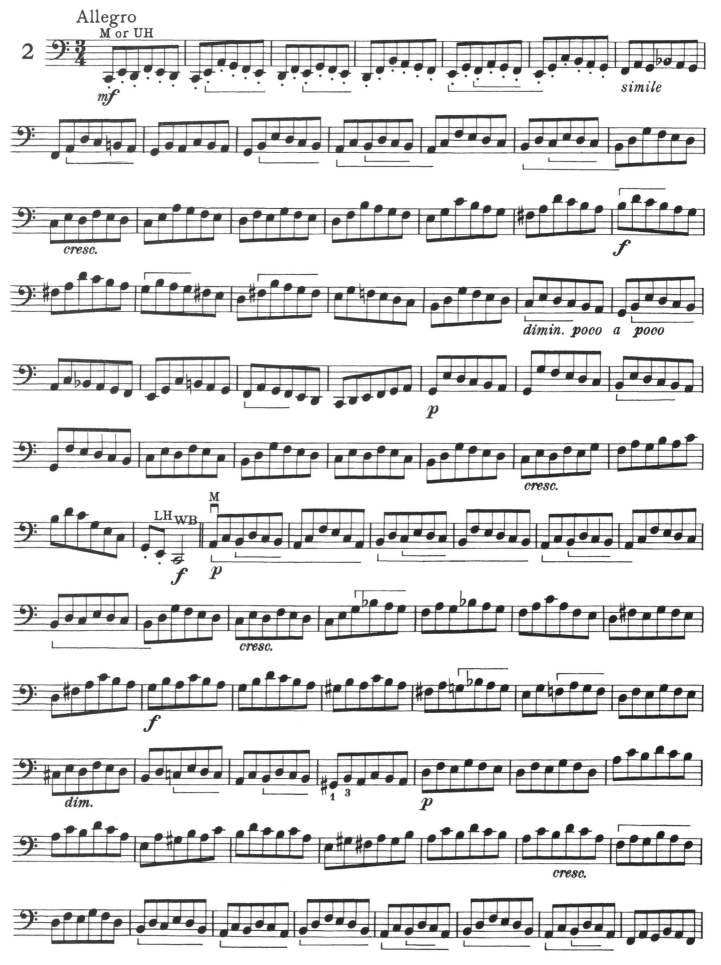

Allegro

4

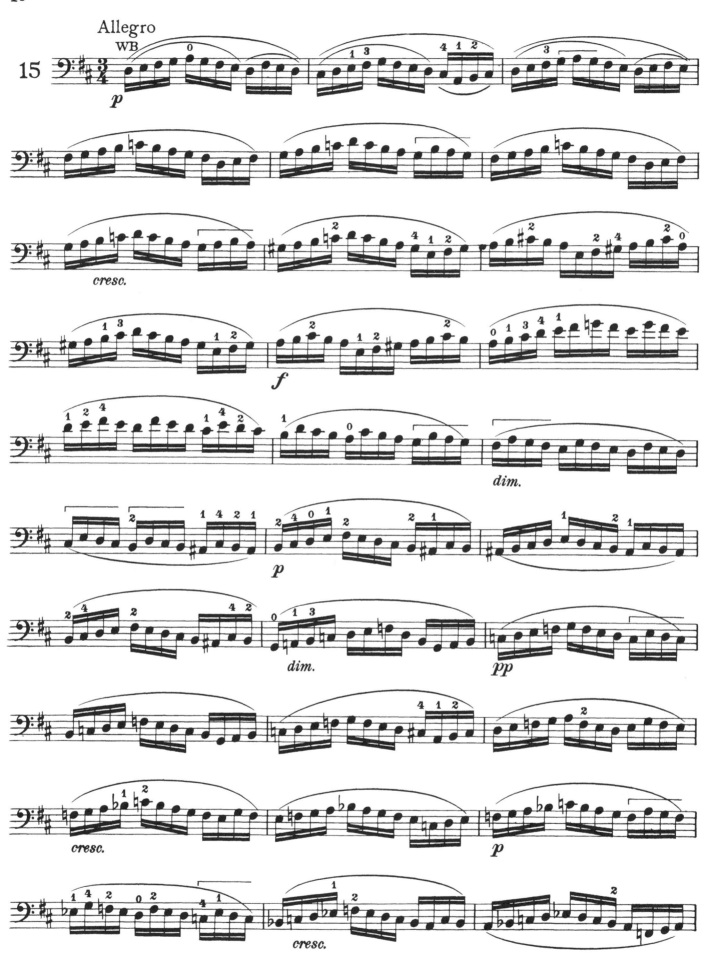

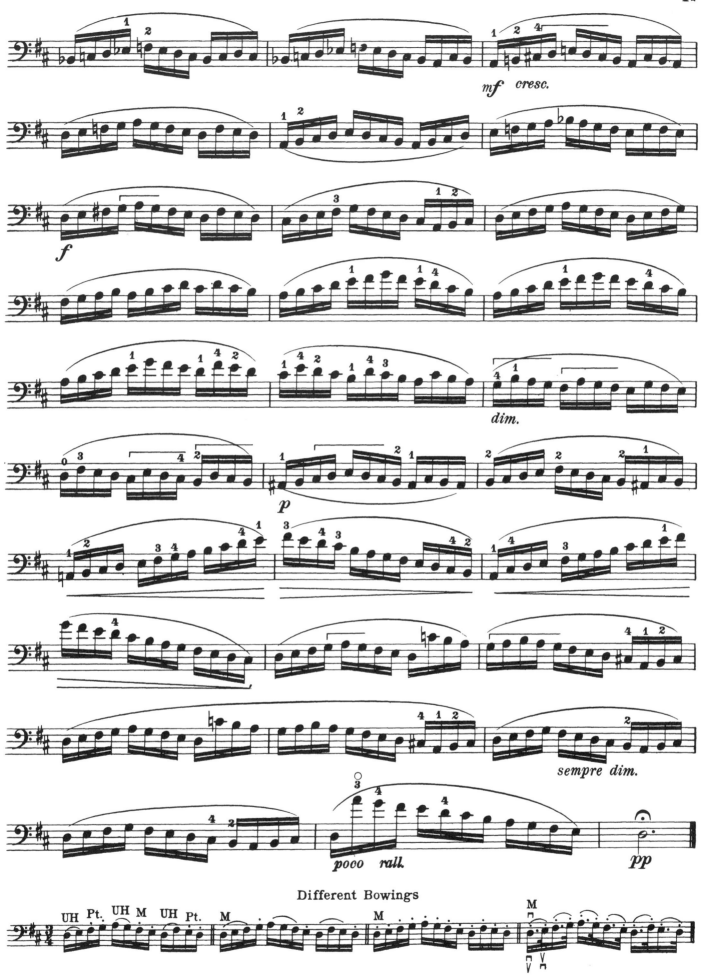

Different Bowings

Maestoso

16

Other Bowings

22

19

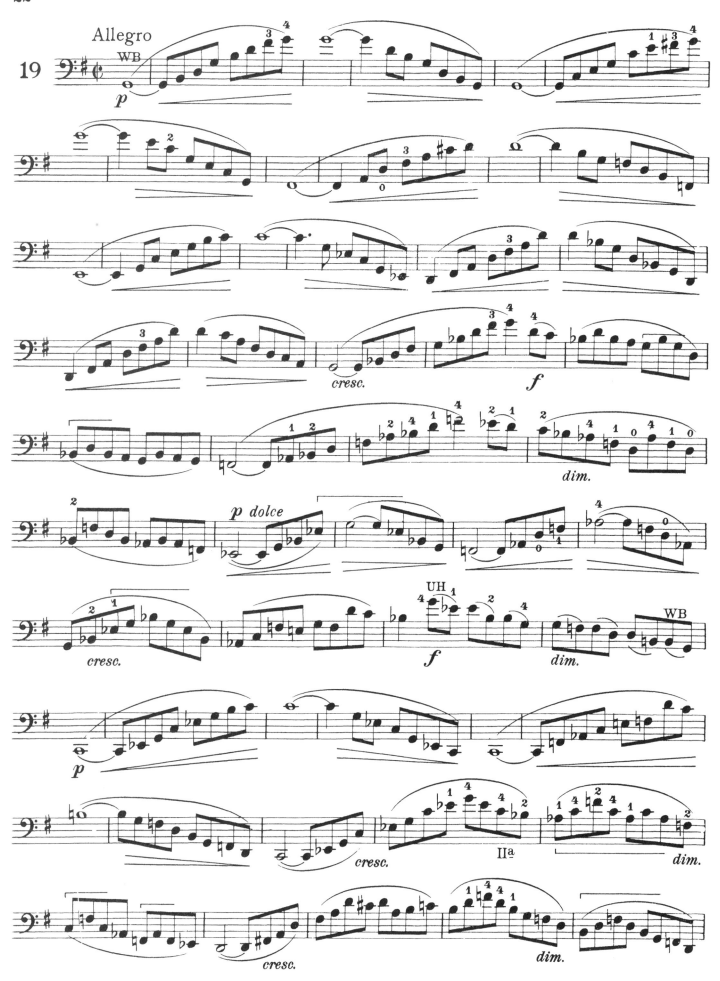

26746

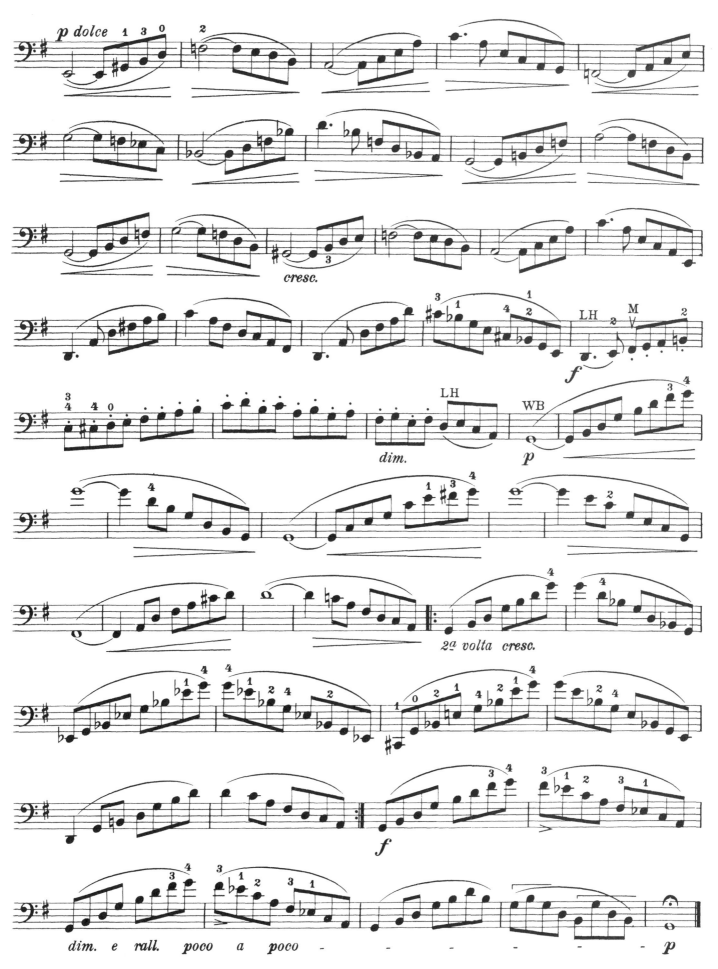

Allegro non troppo

22

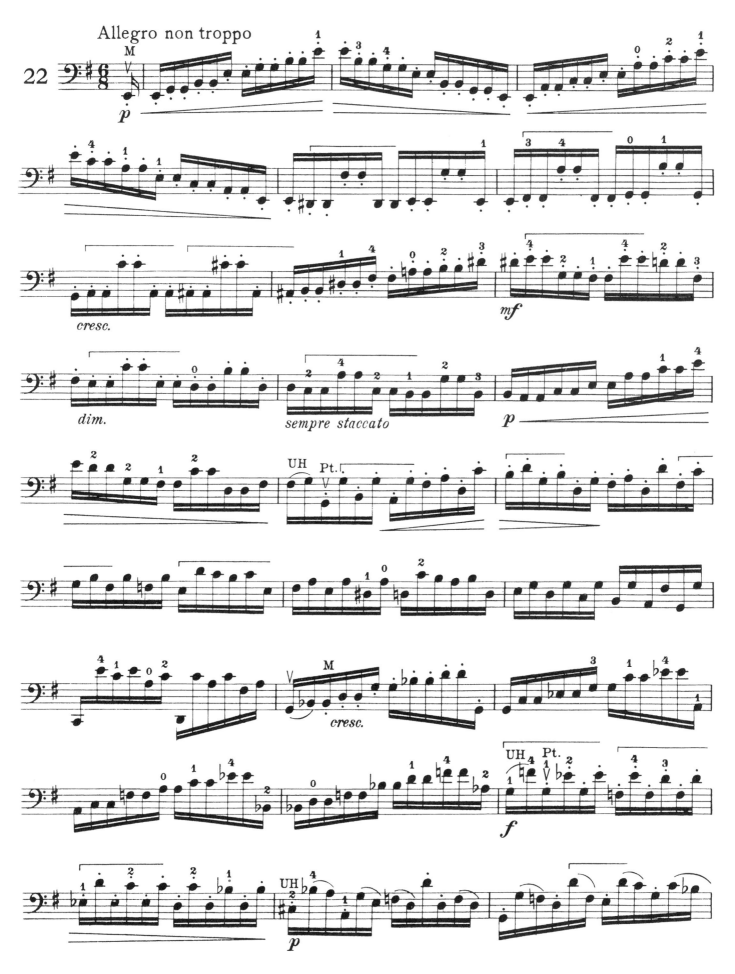

Allegro

23

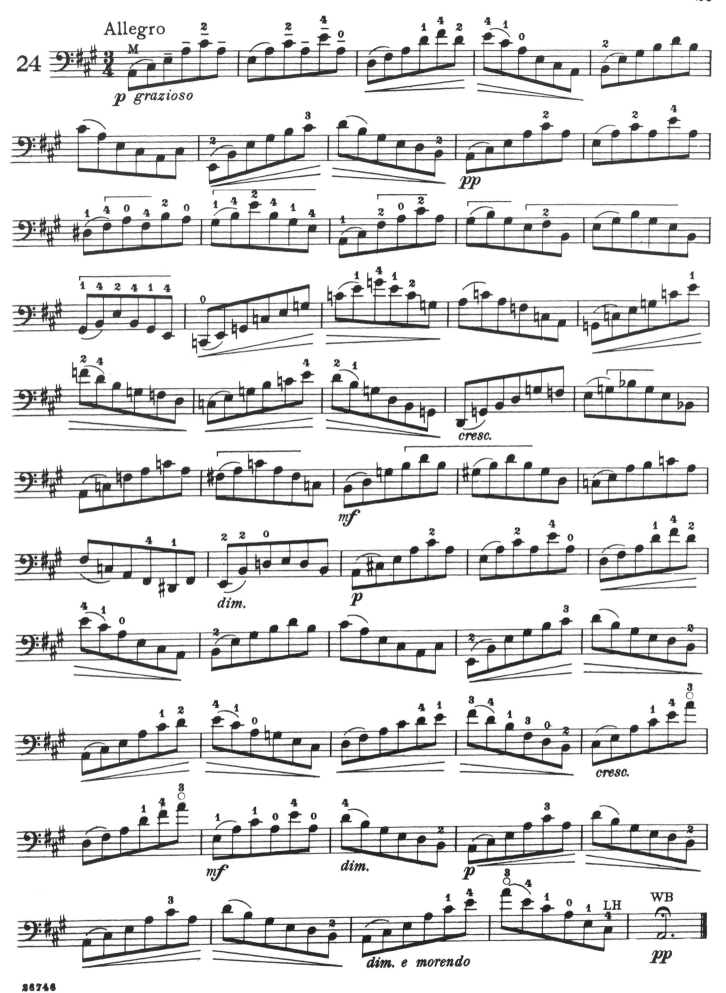

Allegro ma non troppo

Arpeggios

Other Bowings

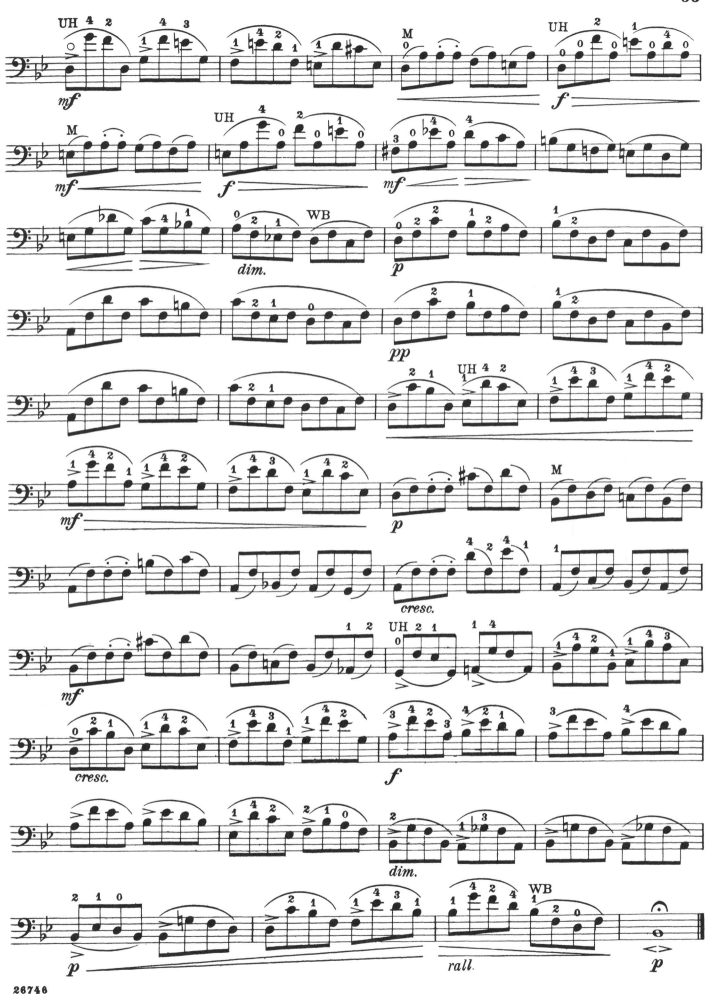

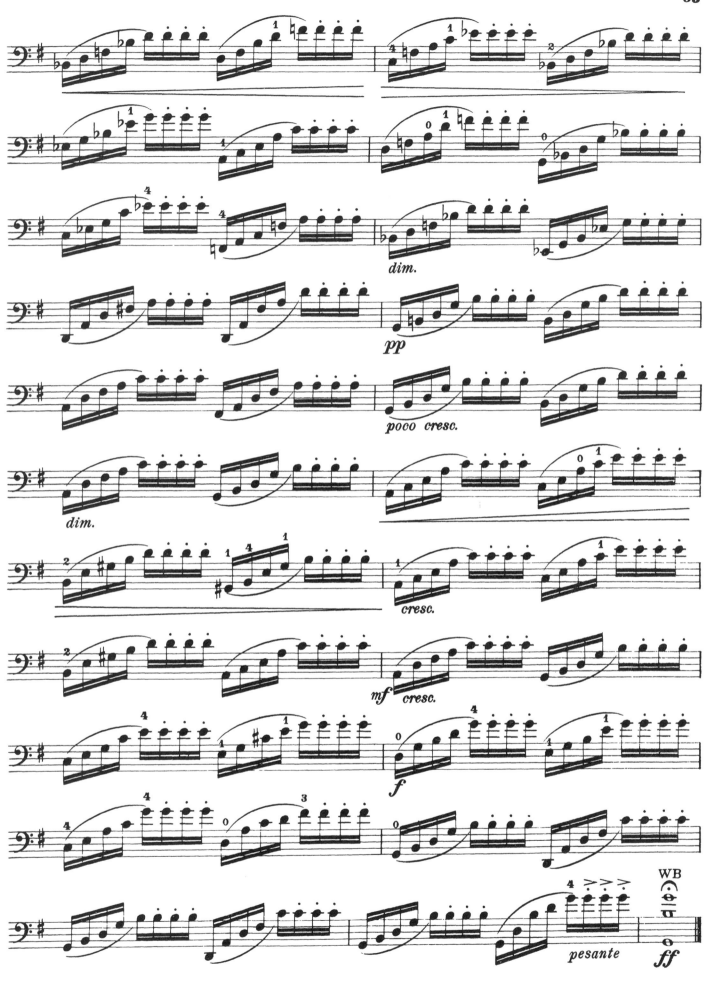

Allegro

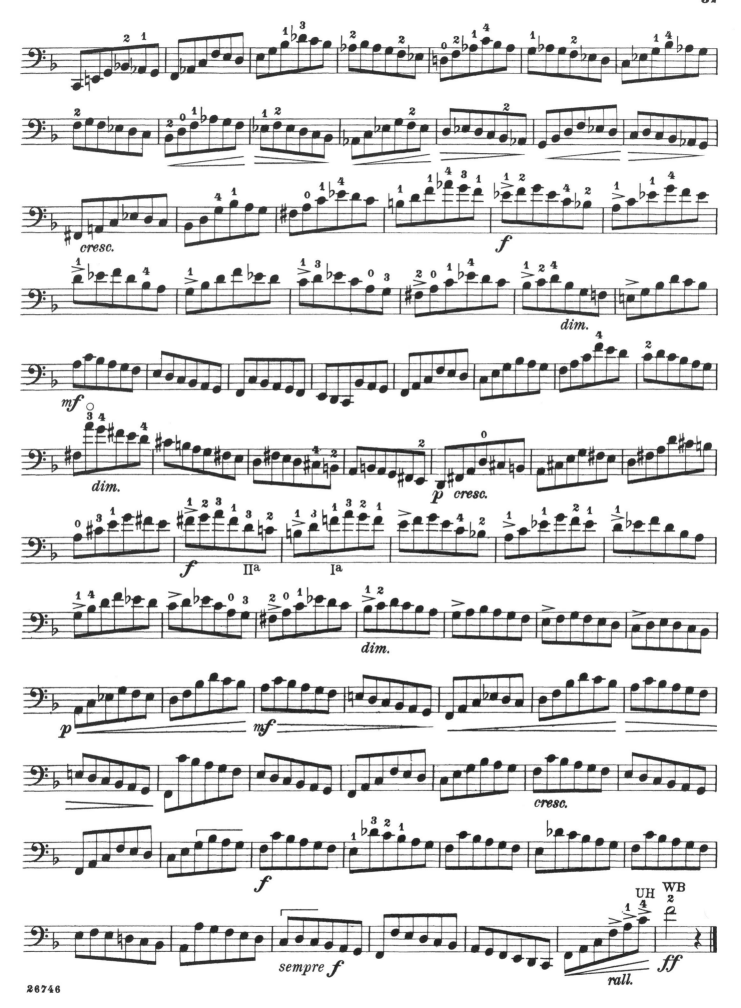

26746

Allegro non troppo

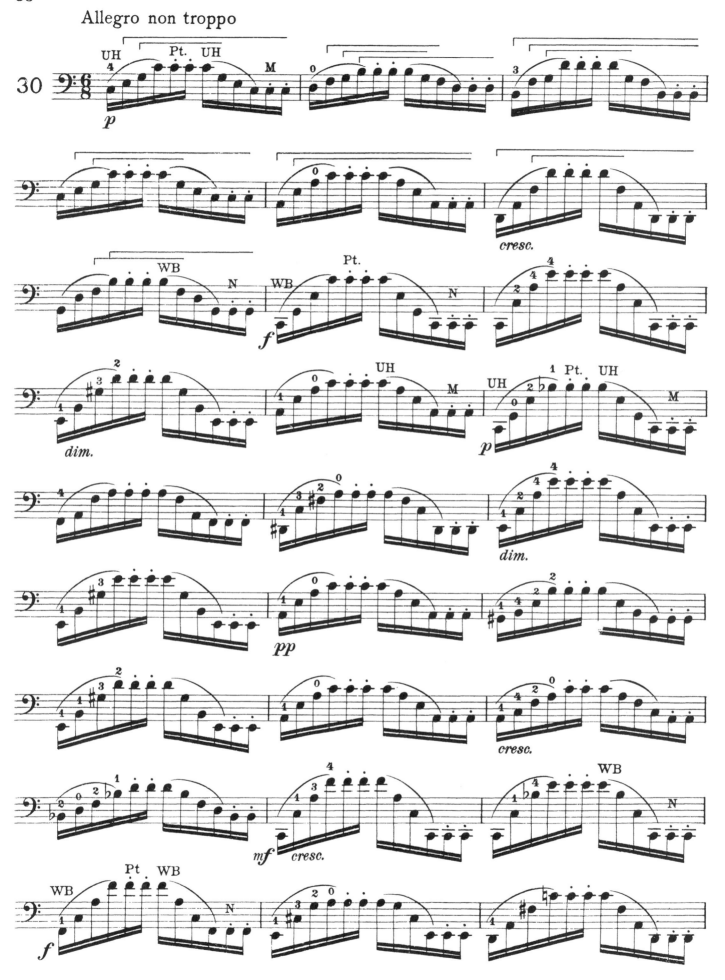

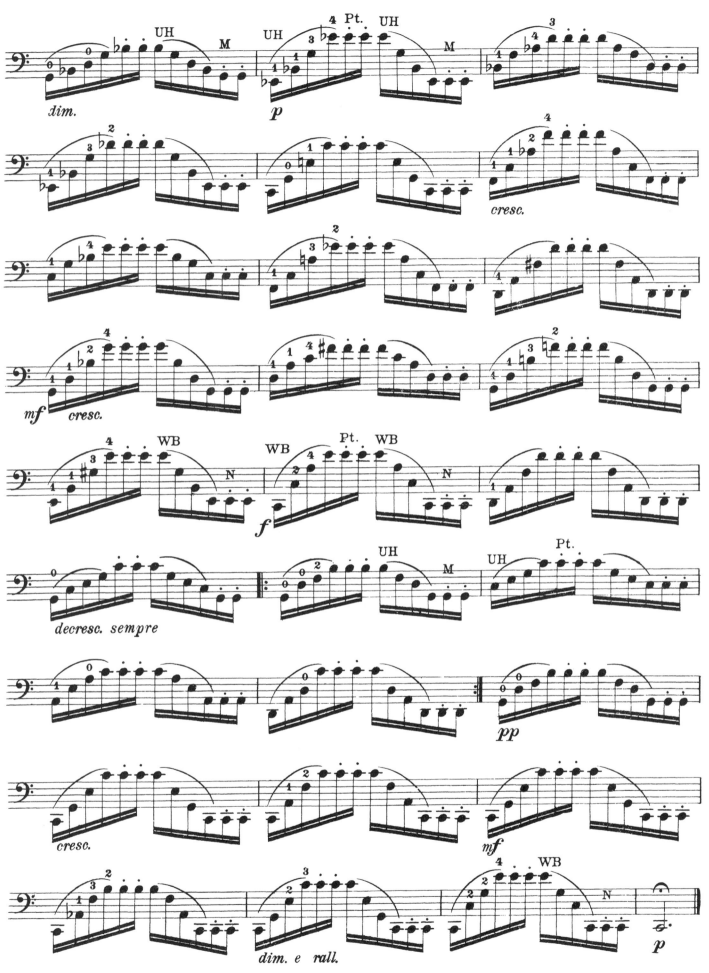

40

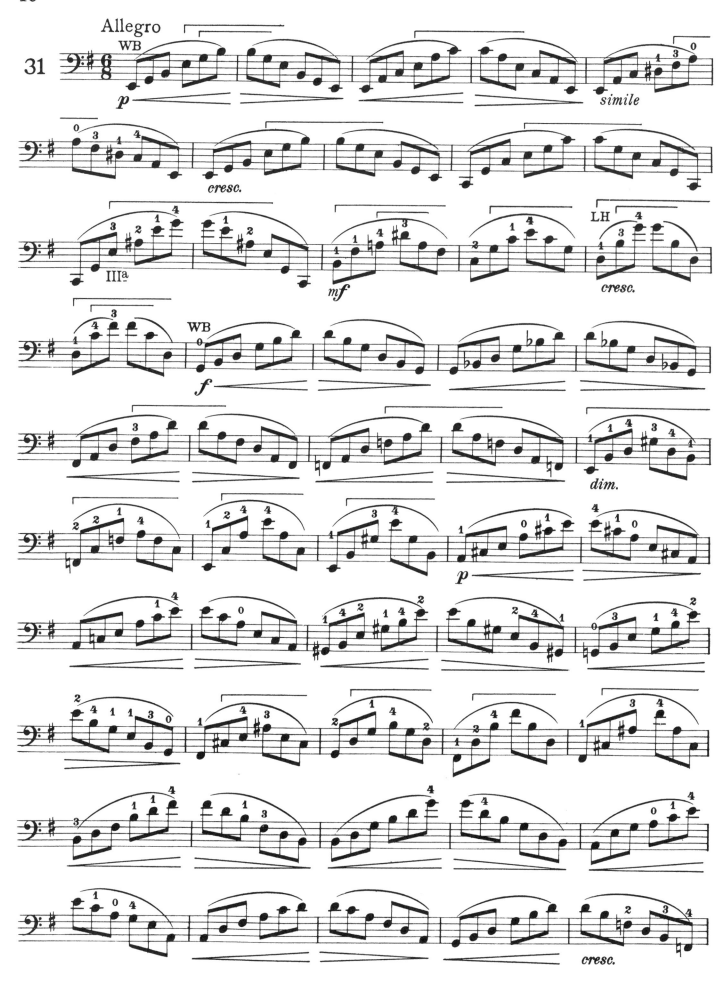

26746

43

26746

Allegro non troppo

33

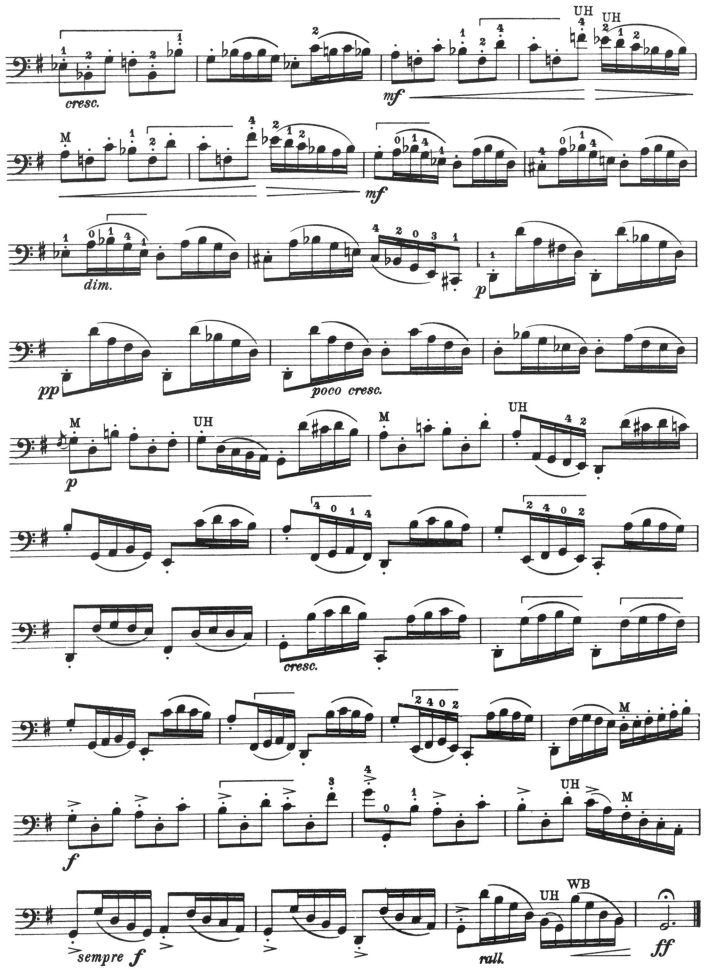

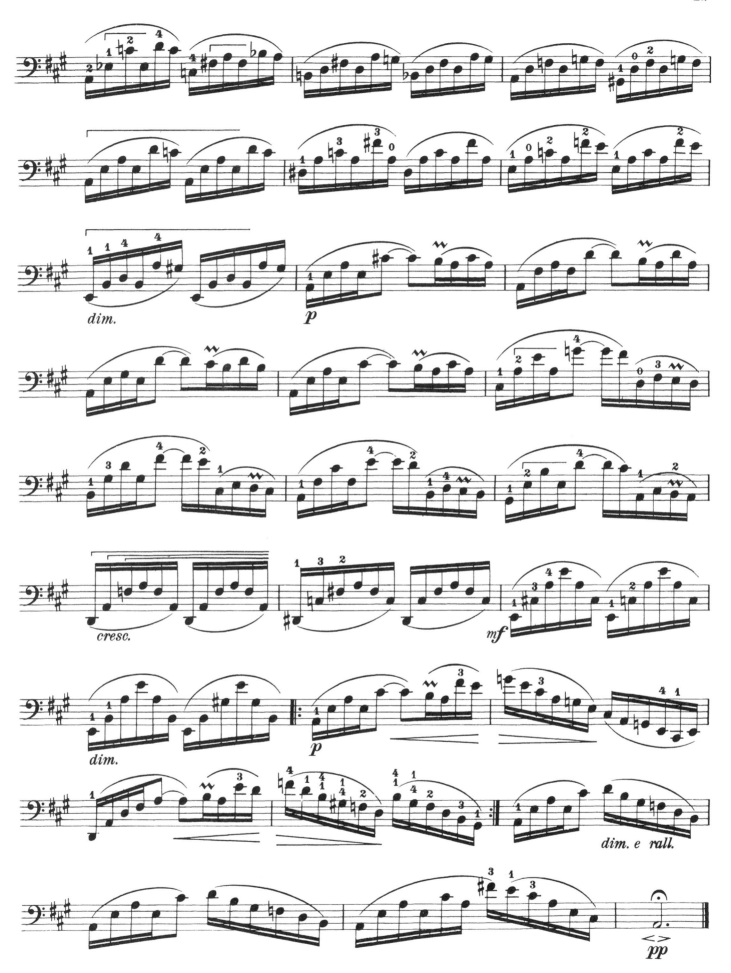